W9-DHG-586

# WHAT IS MONEY?

Claire Llewellyn
illustrated by Mike Gordon

WINDMILL BOOKS

Published in 2017 by **Windmill Books**,
an Imprint of Rosen Publishing
29 East 21st Street, New York, NY 10010


Senior editor: Camilla Lloyd
Designer: Paul Cherrill
Digital Color: Carl Gordon

Cataloging-in-Publication Data
Names: Llewellyn, Claire.
Title: What is money? / Claire Llewellyn and Mike Gordon.
Description: New York : Windmill Books, 2017. | Series: Your money | Includes index.
Identifiers: ISBN 9781499482003 (pbk.) | ISBN 9781499482010 (library bound) |
ISBN 9781508193111 (6 pack)
Subjects: LCSH: Money--Juvenile literature.
Classification: LCC HG221.5 L56 2017 | DDC 332.4--dc23

Manufactured in the United States of America
CPSIA Compliance Information: Batch #BW17PK: For Further Information contact
Rosen Publishing, New York, New York at 1-800-237-9932

# WHAT IS MONEY?

Written by
Claire Llewellyn

Illustrated by
Mike Gordon

We all use money from time
to time to buy things like food ...

... or to pay for a ride.

Money is made up of coins and bills.
They come in different colors, shapes and sizes.
And there are numbers on them, too.

This makes it easy
to count your money.

How much money do you have?

Mom gives me 50¢
if I wash the dog.

Sometimes money comes when you expect it. Sometimes it's a surprise.

It may be a special treat...

... or a way of saying "Well done!"...

... or maybe just a lucky find.

You always need to take care with money because it is very easy to lose ...

... and when it's gone, you can't get it back.

So always keep your money in a safe place.

If you have to carry it around, make sure you put it in a purse or wallet and ask a grown-up to look after it for you.

You can use your money to buy things.
Before you do, think carefully
about what you really want.

X-RAY SPECS

It's easy to spend it
on the wrong thing.

Sometimes you don't have enough money to buy the thing you want.

If you wait and save your money, little by little, your money will grow.

Maybe, one day, you can buy what you wanted after all.

But, remember, it's not THINGS
that make us happy.

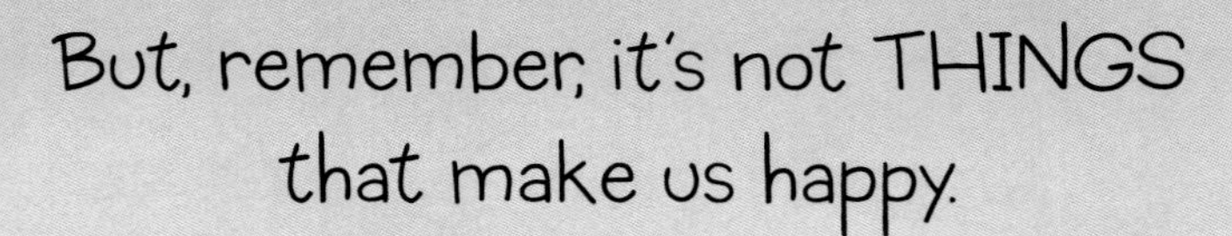

or playing with your friends.
And, luckily, times like these are fabulous, fun and FREE!

# Notes for Parents and Teachers

We all need to be able to manage our money and make financial decisions. The four books in the *Your Money* series are intended as a first step along this path. Based on children's everyday lives, the series is a lighthearted introduction to money, everyday financial transactions, planning and saving and financial choices.

*What Is Money?* introduces the concept of money, and familiarizes readers with bills and coins. It looks at the different ways we can get money and how we use it to spend or save. It explains why we should look after our money and what happens when we lose it.

## Suggested follow-up activities

• Do a survey to assess where most children get their money from. How many get pocket money? How many get presents from other family members? How many do chores for cash? Present the results as a pictogram.

• Cut out pictures of people (e.g. children, teenagers, retired people, tradespeople, professionals) from catalogues or magazines. Prepare some possible captions, explaining where each person gets his or her money from – e.g. "I go to work every day;" "I work on Saturdays;" "I get money on my birthday;" "I have a pension." Ask children to choose the best caption for each person.

- Give children lots of different bills and coins. Allow them to familiarize themselves with them. Which is the most valuable coin or bill? Which is the least valuable? What color are the bills and coins? What pictures are on them? What is written on them? Can they say how much each one is worth?

- Make a collection of different currencies from around the world. What are they called? Can the children find out where they are used and mark this on a map? Do they know what they are worth?

- Set up a shop and ask children to stick prices on items for sale. Give them money to handle. Get them to role-play buying and selling, and to calculate change.

- Make a collection of items for children to "buy." Ask them to price them at under 50¢. Say that each child has $1 to spend and must choose two items. How much change will they get from their $1?

- Look for different poems and stories about money. Why not try to write one of your own?

- Money is always on the move. Have children devise a story about a day in the life of a dollar bill.

## BOOKS TO READ

*Learning About Money: Saving Money* by Mary Firestone
(First Fact Books, 2004)

*Using Money* by Rebecca Rissman
(Heinemann Library, 2010)

## WEBSITES

For web resources related to the subject of this book, go to:
**www.windmillbooks.com/weblinks** and select this book's title.

## INDEX

bills 6
birthday money 8
buying 4, 16, 18, 19

coins 6

food 4

money 4, 6, 7, 8, 9, 10, 11, 12,
13, 14, 16, 17, 18, 19

playing 20, 21
pocket money 8
purse 15

ride 5

saving 19
spending 17

treat 10